MEN-AT-ARMS SERIES

EDITOR: MARTIN WIND

The Army of Northern Virginia

Text by

PHILIP R. N. KATCHER

Colour plates by

MICHAEL YOUENS

OSPREY PUBLISHING LONDON

Published in 1975 by
Osprey Publishing Ltd
59 Grosvenor Street, London, W1X 9DA
© Copyright 1975 Osprey Publishing Ltd
Reprinted 1984, 1985, 1986, 1987 (twice), 1988, 1989

ISBN 0 85045 210 4

Filmset in Great Britain
Printed in Hong Kong

INTRODUCTION

The Army of Northern Virginia was born under fire.

'Shot and shell began to come thick and fast as, surmounting the rise of the hill, we arrived in plain view of the Yankees, and halfway across the field men began to drop, wounded or dead, from the ranks.' The writer is Private J.B. Polley, 4th Texas Regiment. The day is 27 June 1862, the day General Robert E. Lee assumed command of troops driving the Federal Army of the Potomac from the Confederate capital of Richmond, Virginia. The day he first officially designated those troops the Army of Northern Virginia.

'We passed over two regiments – said to have been Virginians – who, protected by a depression of the ground, were apparently afraid either to advance or retreat. At the crest of the hill [Texas General John B.] Hood shouted rapidly the orders, "Fix bayonets! Make ready! Aim! Fire! Charge!" The timber between us and the enemy hid them from view, but we pulled triggers nevertheless, and rushed down the hill into and across the branch, at the Yankees in the first line of breastworks. They waited not for the onset, but fled like a flock of sheep, carrying with them their supports in the second and third lines. Reaching the road which ran along the summit of the hill beyond the branch, and looking to our left, we could see large bodies of the enemy in full retreat, but they were so far behind us that, mistaken for our own troops, not a shot was fired at them. . . .'

The Army of Northern Virginia might have sprung into being, under fire, already organized and battle-tested, but that only happened after the war was already a year old. The men, companies and regiments which first came to the defence of their own states and the new Confederate States of America certainly did not arrive hardened and combat-ready.

Uniforms and Insignia

An English observer, at the war's outset in 1861, reported home that 'The appearance which a regiment presents on parade is remarkable to the eye of a European. Many are composed of companies who have uniforms of different colours; but in these cases there is always some distinctive

General Robert E. Lee

A Tennessee regiment joins the Army of Northern Virginia in early 1861. Note the tomahawks in their belts and the 'Stars and Bars' Confederate flag

badge by which their particular corps can be easily told. This defect, consequent upon the companies being raised in different neighbourhoods, is being quickly remedied, and we saw numerous regiments, which had later arrived, whose dress was all that the Horse Guards could desire.'

The Confederate Army had been created, as the Confederacy itself was being created, from state organizations. Some had been fancy, pre-war militia units, like the 1st Virginia Regiment, the Washington Artillery of Louisiana or the Clinch Rifles of Georgia. These, of course, already had uniforms, accoutrements and weapons, and were drilled. Others, also socially élite, formed units at the war's beginning and nothing was too good for them. The Georgia Hussars in 1861 spent $25,000 on their initial outfits.

At the war's beginning, too, troops who enlisted for twelve months were supposed to be fully equipped by the Confederate Government – against the advice of professional officers like Lee who had left the U.S. Army to side with their states. Not that there was all that much equipment to go round. Company commanders who wrote to the government when it was still in Montgomery, Alabama, before it moved to Richmond, were told that volunteers should furnish their own clothes.

Those in pre-war or city units usually received uniforms, while their rural brothers – who made up the majority of the army – usually had only what they brought from home. One point in common, however, was noted by the English observer: 'Besides the Enfield rifle, most of the privates in the army carry at least one revolver and a bowie knife: these are invariably kept bright and in good condition. . . .'

A veteran of the Richmond Howitzers, Francis McCarthy, recalled: 'Many, expecting terrific hand-to-hand encounters, carried revolvers, and even bowie knives. . . . Revolvers were found to be about as useless and heavy lumber as a private soldier could carry, and early in the war were sent home. . . .'

The volunteer of 1861 had brought other equipment to the field, too. Wrote McCarthy: 'The volunteer of 1861 made extensive preparations for the field. Boots, he thought, were an absolute necessity, and the heavier the soles and longer the tops the better. His pants were stuffed inside the tops of his boots, of course. . . . Experience soon demonstrated that boots were not agreeable on a long march. They were heavy and irksome, and when the heels were worn a little one-sided, the wearer would find his ankle twisted nearly out of joint by every unevenness of the road. When thoroughly wet, it was a laborious undertaking to get them off, and worse to get them on in time to answer the morning roll-call. And so good, strong brogues or brogans with broad bottoms and big, flat heels succeeded the boots. . . .'

'A double-breasted coat, heavily wadded, with two rows of big, brass buttons, and a long skirt was considered comfortable. A short-waisted and single-breasted jacket usurped the place of the long-tailed coat and became universal. The enemy noticed this peculiarity, and called the Confederates "gray jackets".

'A small stiff cap with a narrow brim took the place of the comfortable felt, or the towering tile worn in civil life. . . . Caps were destined to hold out longer than some other uncomfortable things, but they finally yielded to the demands of comfort and common sense, and a good soft felt hat was worn instead.'

Another artilleryman, the commander of the Staunton Artillery, wrote about his men early in 1861 that 'I had provided them with red flannel shirts at Harper's Ferry, because our uniforms were too fine for camp life and for service in the field.'

The newly arrived recruits, or separate companies, were quickly assigned to regiments, ten companies to a regiment. Each company was supposed to have a captain, a first and a second lieutenant, and orderly (or first) sergeant, four sergeants, eight corporals, two musicians and eighty-two privates. Besides them, the regiment had a colonel, a lieutenant-colonel, a major, an adjutant, a quartermaster, a surgeon and his assistant. There was also a sergeant-major, a quartermaster-sergeant, a commissary sergeant and a hospital steward. Most regiments, too, took brass bands with them to war, although it was said the quality of their music fell off badly towards 1865.

The Confederate Army made an attempt to avoid reducing regiments, as losses made them too small to be effective while raising new ones, by sending recruiters to each regiment's home area and feeding recruits into it throughout the war. Thus, unit *esprit de corps* was maintained to the end in most regiments. Furthermore, the recruits and conscripts found themselves in units with a majority of seasoned veterans, which greatly steadied them in action. It was rarely that a totally inexperienced bunch of men was sent against the enemy after the first year or so of war.

On the other hand, regiments and even brigades and divisions, as much as possible, were organized strictly along state lines. General Joseph Johnston, commanding the army before Lee, wrote in September 1861 about the 1st Virginia Cavalry: 'The regiment so far is exclusively Virginian. By all means keep it so, where it can be done without prejudicing other respects. State pride excites a generous emulation in the Army, which is of inappreciable value in its effects on the spirit of the troops.' Such an attitude may have added to the men's unit pride, but it also greatly damaged the overall army, in that the states felt responsible for their regiments only. When Lee's ragged men surrendered in 1865, North Carolina had 92,000 new uniforms in its warehouses – uniforms they would issue to North Carolinians only.

The Confederate of 1861 was generally armed with a bowie knife like this one, although they were soon discarded. (Author's collection)

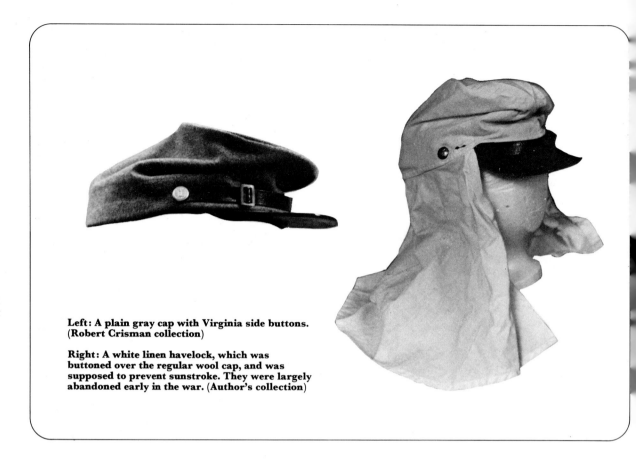

Left: A plain gray cap with Virginia side buttons. (Robert Crisman collection)

Right: A white linen havelock, which was buttoned over the regular wool cap, and was supposed to prevent sunstroke. They were largely abandoned early in the war. (Author's collection)

Another idea which seemed good at the time, but led to more trouble than it was worth, was conscription. 'With the Spring [of 1862] came the end of the term of enlistment of many of the soldiers', wrote a South Carolina artillery officer. 'Most of them went home to visit their families. The majority soon re-enlisted, but often in new commands; some did not re-enlist at all, others did much later. Many of the regiments reorganized with new officers. The general effect was to break up very much the organization of the army.'

The twelve-month men were theoretically gone, but not in reality. For in April 1862 Congress passed the Conscription Act, stating, among other things, that all men between eighteen and thirty-five who enlisted for one year would be conscripted to serve throughout the war. Such an Act was highly unpopular with the men, even those wanting to re-enlist anyway, because it took away their status of 'volunteer' and appeared to force them to serve. Conscripts were generally distrusted by volunteers.

Private Polley recalled at Fredericksburg: 'Only two regiments of our division were engaged in any undertaking that might be called a battle. These were the Fifty-seventh and Fifty-fourth North Carolina regiments composed of conscripts – young men under twenty and old men – all dressed in homespun, and presenting to the fastidious eye of us veterans a very unsoldierly appearance.' The two regiments, much to Polley's surprise, did quite well, and drove out a Union force larger than themselves.

Actually, a fastidious, soldierly eye might even find some flaws in the veterans' dress. Therefore, it was one of the first matters of business, once an army was created, to design and order a standard uniform. A board of officers, therefore, met in Richmond to do just that. According to a general who served on it, 'the intention of the board was to adopt a tunic like the short, close-fitting Austrian garment, but it went by default. The officers would have none of it. They took the familiar cut of frock coat with a good length of tail.'

The coat which was acceptable for a general

Second Lieutenant J. B. Washington, aide to General Johnston, sits with his old West Point classmate, Second Lieutenant G. A. Custer, 5th U.S. Cavalry, on the day Washington was captured, 31 May 1862. Note the trim on his coat, his pockets and the U.S. shoulder-strap rank insignia

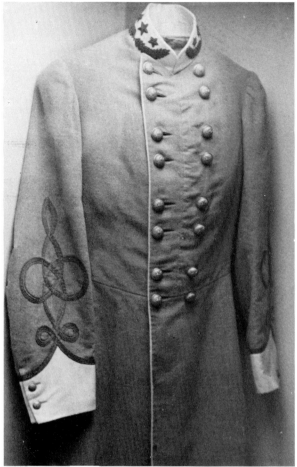

Uniform coat of Brigadier-General James Pettigrew. (Gettysburg National Military Park)

officer (all Confederate generals wore identical uniforms regardless of grade) had 'two rows of buttons on the breast, eight in each row, placed in pairs; the distance between the rows four inches at top and three inches at bottom; stand-up collar, to rise no higher than to permit the chin to turn freely over it; to hook in front at the bottom, and slope thence up and backward, at an angle of thirty degrees, on each side; cuffs two and a half inches deep on the underside, there to be buttoned with three small buttons, and sloped upwards to a point at a distance of four inches from the end of the sleeve; pockets in the folds of the skirt, with one button at the hip and one at the end of each pocket, making four buttons on the back and skirt of the tunic, the hip buttons to range with the lowest breast buttons.'

All other officers were to have identical coats, only with seven evenly placed buttons on them.

Other ranks had the same dress coat, but with only two buttons on each cuff and 'narrow lining in the skirts of the tunic of gray material'. For fatigue they could wear '. . . a light gray blouse, double breasted, with two rows of small buttons, seven in each row; small turnover collar . . .'.

Cuffs and collar were facing colours, and by regulation 'The facings for General officers, and for officers of the Adjutant General's Department, Quartermaster General's Department, Commissary General's Department, and the Engineers will be buff. The tunic of all officers to be edged throughout with the facings designated: Medical Department – black; Artillery – red; Cavalry – yellow; Infantry – light blue.'

Trousers were to be sky-blue for regimental officers and other ranks, and dark blue for all other officers. Generals were to have two stripes of gold lace on their trousers, other officers one stripe, and regimental officers and non-commissioned officers a stripe of their facing colour.

The cap was originally to be a gray copy of the French *képi* with a red, sky-blue or yellow pompon for the different branches. On 24 January 1862, however, the cap was changed. Still a *képi*, it was now to have a dark blue band round the bottom, with the sides and crown of the facing colour. Other ranks' caps were to have 'the number of the regiment . . . worn in front, in yellow metal'. Officers were to have stripes of gold lace, according to rank, up the back, front and sides. Generals were to have four gold stripes, field officers three, captains two, and lieutenants one. Besides the stripes up the sides, '. . . the center of the crown [is] to be embroidered with the same number of braids'.

The same number of braids were also worn, in the form of an 'Austrian knot', on officers' coat sleeves.

Also, according to regulation, 'In hot weather, a white duck, or linen cover, known as a havelock, will be worn – the apron to fall behind, so as to protect the ears and neck from the rays of the sun. In winter, in bad weather, an oilskin cover will be worn, with an apron to fall over the coat collar.' Havelocks were initially popular, but rapidly found better use as coffee-strainers and gun patches. The oilskin covers were virtually figments of the board's imagination.

'Stonewall' Jackson, a contemporary woodcut

North Carolina's other ranks were to wear '. . . a sack coat of gray cloth [of North Carolina manufacture] extending halfway down the thigh, and made loose, with falling collar, and an inside pocket on each breast, six coat buttons down the front, commencing at the throat; a strip of cloth sewed on each shoulder, extending from the base of the collar to the shoulder seam, an inch and a half wide at the base of the collar, and two inches wide at the shoulder; this strip will be of black cloth for Infantry, red for Artillery and yellow for Cavalry.' Musicians, who had no special uniforms under Confederate regulations, were to wear their facing colours as horizontal bars across their chests. Generals were to have blue trousers, but all other officers and other ranks were to have gray trousers with black, red or yellow stripes down their legs. Gray forage caps, floppy versions of the *képi*, were to be worn by all ranks for fatigue and a gray felt hat for dress.

Officers were to wear U.S. Army rank insignia, while non-commissioned ranks were distinguished by chevrons worn on both arms. A sergeant-major had three bars and three arcs, a quartermaster-sergeant had three bars and three ties, while a commissary sergeant had three bars and a star. An orderly sergeant had three bars and a lozenge. Each sergeant had three bars, and each corporal, two. All Confederates, in fact, used this, non-commissioned-officer insignia system.

There is little indication, however, that even state dress regulations were followed, save in the matter of rank insignia. Lieutenant-Colonel A. J. L. Fremantle, Coldstream Guards, visited the army in 1863 and reported on it with the eye of a trained soldier: 'The men were good-sized, healthy and well clothed, although without any attempt at uniformity in colour or cut, but nearly all were dressed either in gray or brown coats and felt hats.

'I was told that even if a regiment was clothed in proper uniform by the government, it would become parti-coloured again in a week, as the soldiers preferred wearing the coarse homespun jackets and trousers made by their mothers and sisters at home. The generals very wisely allow them to please themselves in this respect, and insist only upon their arms and accoutrements being kept in proper order. Most of the officers

Actually, most of this fancy regulation uniform was little more than a figment of the board's imagination rather than anything which actually saw service. To begin with, many of the regiments had already made up their own dress regulations and wore their old uniforms. Then many states set up their own regulations, and made uniforms more to follow them than the army-wide regulations.

North Carolina, for example, had a board of its officers who set up their own regulations on 23 May 1861. Its officers were to wear '. . . a frock coat, the skirt to extend from two-thirds to three-quarters the distance from the top of the hips to the bend of the knee, single-breasted for Captains and Lieutenants, double-breasted for all other grades – of North Carolina gray cloth for all Regimental Officers – of dark blue cloth for General Officers and Officers of the General Staff.'

A contemporary official print of, from left, a general, an adjutant-general and a colonel of engineers.

A colonel, lieutenant-colonel and captain of artillery.

A colonel, captain and first lieutenant of infantry.

A sergeant, private and musician of cavalry. (Author's collection)

were dressed in uniform which is neat and service-able – a bluish-gray frock coat of a colour similar to the Austrian *jägers*. The infantry wear blue facings, the artillery red, the doctors black, the staff white, and the cavalry yellow; so it is [also] impossible to mistake his rank. A second lieutenant, first lieutenant, and captain, wear respectively one, two and three bars on the collar. A major, lieutenant-colonel and colonel wear one, two and three stars on the collar.'

Officers, generally, did try to conform to regulation dress. Even so, field use tended to make

them a bit less smart than they were supposed to appear. A Light Division company commander wrote home: 'I have my sword, a blanket, haver-sack, canteen, and a change of underclothing in a light knapsack, and let everything else go; for our wagons are always far off – you never can find what you put in them – and as we are continually moving about, I find my load sufficiently heavy without adding to it. When ordered to march, I am at the head of my company, heavily laden as any. . . .'

The typical private, as described by one of

hem, was even more unmilitary in appearance: Around the upper part of the face is a fringe of unkempt hair, and above this is an old wool hat worn and weatherbeaten, and the flaccid brim of which falls limp upon the shoulders behind, and is folded back in front against the elongated and crumpled crown. Over a soiled shirt, which is unbuttoned at the collar, is a ragged gray jacket that does not reach the hips, with sleeves some inches too short. Below this trousers of a non-descript color, without form and almost void, are held in place by a leather belt, to which is attached the cartridge-box that rests behind the right hip, and the bayonet scabbard that dangles on the left.

'Just above the ankles of each trouser leg is tied closely; and, behind, reaches of dirty socks disappear into a pair of badly used and curiously contorted shoes. Between the jacket and the waist-band of the trousers, or the supporting belt, there appears a puffy display of cotton shirt which works out further with every hitch made by Johnny in his efforts to keep his trousers in place. Across his body from his left shoulder there is a roll of threadbare blanket, the ends tied together resting on or falling below the right hip. This is Johnny's bed. Within this roll is a shirt, his only extra article of clothing.'

As Colonel Fremantle was told, most soldiers preferred clothing from home. One Alabamian wrote home in 1864: 'I send you a couple of shirts and a pair of drawers. Use them as you please. I had rather wear your make. The reason I drew them was that they are so much cheaper than you can make them. You can use them in making clothes for the children.' One Virginian practically made a business of selling his home-made clothes. He wrote home: 'I have sold my pants, vest, shoes and drawers for sixty-one dollars so you can see I am flush again. . . . You will have to make me more pants and drawers, if you can raise the material make two pair of pants and four pair of drawers and I will have a pair of pants and two pair of drawers for sale and in that way will get mine clear . . . if you could make up a good supply of pants, vests, shirts and drawers, I could be detailed out to come after them.'

Another source of supply – probably the most important one of all in all areas of Confederate

Many Confederates wore blouses with lay-down collars. Such blouses were, in fact, regulation among North Carolina troops. (Author's collection)

supply – was the Federal Government. It was a saying in the army that all a Yankee was worth was his shoes, and after Fredericksburg the story went round how a Confederate soldier stopped to pull off the boots of a Union officer supposed dead. Suddenly, in the midst of pulling off the first boot, the 'corpse' weakly raised his head and cursed the rebel for robbing the wounded. 'Beg pardon, sir,' replied the Confederate as he nonchalantly walked away, 'I thought you had gone above.'

In many companies the combination of a gray or brown jacket and Union sky-blue trousers was so common as to be almost regulation. The trouble began, of course, when the men showed in virtually complete regulation Federal uniform. One Confederate commander was forced to order in December 1864: 'All men and officers belonging to this command who have blue Yankee overcoats and clothing who do not have them dyed by the 20th Inst *The Coats Especially* will be taken from them. . . .'

The problem in mixing up which side was which was obvious, and could be fatal. An artillery colonel recalled, just before the Wilderness: 'Jenkin's Brigade was one of those which had recently returned from the South, and the men were dressed in new uniforms made of cloth so dark a gray as to be almost black. Mahone's men, some distance off in the thick underbrush, hearing the cheers and seeing this body of dark-uniformed men, took them for Yankees and fired a volley. Fortunately they fired high, or there would have been a terrible slaughter.'

These troops may have been among those seen as prisoners shortly later by an Ohio lieutenant who wrote: '. . . we had the pleasure of seeing about four thousand prisoners passing us on their way to the rear. They seemed completely surprised, which is a wonder for old troops. As to their appearance, they were all clad in neat gray jackets and pantaloons with entire seats. In contrast we were in rags, scarcely one of us having a complete garment of any sort.'

This must have been virtually the only time when captured Confederates were better dressed than their captors. A Texan wrote in 1864 that 'in this army one hole in the seat of the breeches indicates a captain, two holes a lieutenant, and the seat of the pants all out indicates that the individual is a private'. In the Richmond Howitzers repairs on trouser seats took an artistic flair when one day a cannoneer showed up for morning roll-call with a bright red flannel heart on the seat of his trousers. Each man, thereafter, had to outdo the next with cut-out eagles, horses, cows and cannon. The contest finally ended when one man showed up with a cupid holding out a bow on one side, and on the other a heart pierced by an arrow – all in bright red wool.

The Confederate Soldier

There were a number of reasons for this lack of uniform, besides states' rights and individual choice, and even they cannot all be laid at the government's feet. Lack of responsibility among the individual troops and poor company-grade officers who failed to make sure their men had all the necessary kit in good order accounted for much of the problem. If given anything the men felt was momentarily unnecessary, they simply threw it away. One Georgia captain wrote in early 1863: 'The Company begins to look as ragged as ours ever did, the cause of it is that they have to toat [carry] their extra clothing and rather than toat it they won't have it.' McCarthy wrote that when going on a march 'soldiers commonly threw away the most valuable articles they possessed. Blankets, overcoats, shoes, bread and meat – all gave way to the necessities of the march. . . .'

Such an irresponsible attitude on the men's part created great problems for them and the entire army. Lee, for example, at Mine Run felt he had the Union army in a position where he could have repeated his magnificent manœuvres of Chancellorsville, only to have to withdraw because his men had thrown away their overcoats and couldn't serve well in the cold November weather.

Even the clothes they did keep were poorly cared for – showing again a failure of company officers to insist on as much neatness as possible. McCarthy reported that 'very little washing was done, as a matter of course. Clothes once given up were parted with forever. There were good reasons for this: cold water would not cleanse them or destroy the vermin, and hot water was not always to be had.' Another 'good' reason was given by another Confederate when he wrote home in 1862 that 'soap seems to have given out entirely in the Confederacy & consequently it is almost impossible to have any clean clothes. I am without drawers today both pairs of mine being so dirty that I can't stand them.'

A Georgian in 1864 noted that some half of his company had gone two months without changing clothes and a Texan wrote in 1865 that '. . . something near half of the command has not changed shirts for 4 or 5 months'. Uncleaned clothes, sweaty and filthy, actually rotted away and were worthless much sooner than cared-for uniforms would have been.

Three typical Confederates, captured at Gettysburg

A Confederate infantry camp. Note the barefoot soldiers

McCarthy expressed the overall attitude: 'It was inconvenient to change the underwear too often, and the disposition not to change grew, as the knapsack was found to gall the back and shoulders and weary the man before half the march was accomplished. The better way was to dress out, and wear that outfit until the enemy's knapsack or the folks at home supplied a change. Certainly it did not pay to carry around clean clothes while waiting for the time to use them.'

Such an attitude is rather amazing for soldiers who served four years in an army which gained such a great reputation. Its reputation, however, is that of a hard-fighting army, and not a well-disciplined one. An English visitor in 1862 reported that 'the soldiers of the Southern army were scrambled together in a few months, and the greater part of them never have gone through any regular course of drill, and are, therefore, wanting in the smartness and precision which distinguish good troops in Europe. Men take off their hats instead of saluting; orders are given in a loose

conversational tone, and the gunner in a battery will suggest an opinion to the captain. But though, for these reasons, the troops might not be presentable on parade, a year's hard service has rendered them efficient for the field.'

Colonel Fremantle was rather taken by the nonconformity of the Confederate soldier: '...The Confederate has no ambition to imitate the regular soldier at all. He looks the genuine Rebel; but in spite of his bare feet, his ragged clothes, his old rug, and a toothbrush stuck like a rose in his buttonhole (this toothbrush in the buttonhole is a very common custom, and has a most quaint effect), he has a sort of devil-may-care, reckless, self-confident look, which is decidedly taking.' The Colonel had been at one dress parade where 'before [the] marching past of the brigade, many of the soldiers had taken off their coats and marched past the general in their shirt sleeves, on account of the warmth'.

The typical Confederate was quite proud of his independence. One of them, when writing about he typical private, said: 'He doesn't care whether anyone likes his looks or not. He is the most independent soldier that ever belonged to an organized army. He has respect for authority, and he submits cheerfully to discipline. He is perfectly tractable if properly officered – but quick to resent an official incivility.'

Such a lax discipline was thought to be no problem by Confederate authorities at first. As one of them explained to an English visitor in 1862: 'The very high standard of individual intelligence, moreover, supplies the want of order in a great measure. Things which, in other armies, if not done on a strict rule, would be altogether neglected, somehow "get themselves done" in this volunteer army. . . . The great strength and power of the Southern army lies in the individual resolution of the men.'

All well and good for an army quickly assembled, fighting a few sharp and hard fights, winning and returning home. But leave that same undisciplined bunch of men in the field any length of time, when they have to be clothed, fed, drilled and kept well and alert, and discipline is a vital part of winning any war. It was not until too late that such a discovery was made by Confederate authorities. One important general, Jubal Early, wrote in February 1865, with only two months of life left for the Army of Northern Virginia, that too much dependence had been placed on the soldiers' innate merit as individuals and not enough consideration given on moulding them into effective units. 'Many opportunities', he wrote, 'have been lost and hundreds of valuable lives

Wood-soled shoes were commonly issued, due to a leather shortage. (**Smithsonian Institution**)

have been uselessly sacrificed for the want of a strict observance of discipline.'

How true this was can be seen in Lee's decision at Mine Run, and in an order of September 1864 covering the whole Army of Northern Virginia: 'There is not that spirit of respect for and obedience to general orders which should pervade a military organization. . . . If the orders governing this subject [straggling] were rigorously enforced, thousands of muskets would be heard in every fight that are now never fired.'

Even those officers who saw the necessity for firm discipline had their hands full in enforcing even the slightest amount of it. McCarthy wrote: 'The Confederate soldier was peculiar in that he was ever ready to fight, but never ready to submit

From left, a Virginia button, an artilleryman's button, a rifleman's button, the general service button and the general and staff officer's button. Regulations called for the corps letter on buttons of regimental officers and other ranks. (**Author's collection**)

An infantry corporal's jacket. (Author's collection)

to the routine duty and discipline of the camp or march. The soldiers were determined to be soldiers after their own notions, and do their duty, for the love of it, as they thought best. The officers saw the necessity for doing otherwise, and so the conflict was commenced and maintained to the end.'

The story went round how General Wigfall, commanding Texas troops, came across a guard reclining on a pile of boxes, his musket leaning against a nearby tree. 'What are you doing here, my man?' asked the General.

'Nothin' much, jes' kinder takin' care of this hyar stuff,' replied the private without moving from his reclining position.

'Do you know who I am, sir?'

'Wal, now 'pears like I know your face, but I can't jes' call your name – who is you?'

'I'm General Wigfall.'

Without rising, the soldier stuck out his hand. 'General, I'm pleased to meet you. My name's Jones.'

The General did nothing about the incident Probably there would have been little he really could have done. Officers were initially elected and although examinations for competency were set up for them in 1862, popularity meant the most in retaining one's rank. In December 186? an Act of Congress was passed to encourage re enlistments, which allowed the men to switch units and even branches of the service if they wished Men who had officers who were disciplinarians usually transferred, and those officers, without any commands, ended up being lost to the army Officers, too, who had the misfortune of being foreign or somehow 'different' from the often small-minded, mostly small farmers serving under them, found it almost impossible to work with their troops. One colonel who was Jewish was sent out to command a Texas regiment, but lasted only a few days, as the men did their best to make life impossible for him.

The feeling against all officers ran deep with many troops. A Texan wrote home in 1864 that 'it is only the ones that wear gray coats and Brass Buttons . . . [who] are living better and wear better clothes than they did before the war. I do not blame them for keeping the war up as long as possible . . . most of them are in no danger, they are always in the rear.'

A real cause for this feeling lay in deep-rooted feelings of that mass of people who made up the Confederacy's other ranks. All too often in their letters home they said the officers were treating them like Negroes – and to the poorer farmer being treated like the only class of people they felt superior to – slaves – was to rob them of a major source of necessary ego. Therefore, the strong spirit of independence, with which they treated all orders and discipline, was very much a part of their very being.

The amazing thing, perhaps, is that any stayed in the army at all. A colonel commanding an artillery battalion obtained leave for two of his men who had performed particularly heroic acts. 'Going home', he recalled, 'they found their cabins and their families as they had left them, with fish a-plenty and a better market – the Union soldiers – than they had [previously] known. They took the oath of allegiance and stayed at home. Their families needed them. There was no glory for them

...o cross of a legion of honor. Their duty was to a ...ause they scarce understood; hardship, suffering, ...nd the danger of death were all they had to ...eturn to. The danger and suffering to them and ...heir families were great, their reward invisible. ...Vho can wonder that they stayed home or judge ...hem harshly? I for one cannot. The true wonder ...s that any held out. Many a morning in camp I ...ave read appeal after appeal for leave to go home ...rom good men, who would attach to their ...etitions letters from their wives, with appeals for ...he men to come home to save their families from ...tarvation and cold.' And go home they did, by ...eave or desertion. In February 1865 the Super-...ntendent of the Bureau of Conscription estimated ...onservatively that there were 100,000 deserters. ...The last returns for the Army of Northern Virginia ...howed 160,198 men present for duty – 198,494 ...bsent.

An Alabama private after the war wrote on their defeat: 'What was the cause of it? Skulkers, Cowards, Extortioners and Deserters not the Yankees that makes it worse.'

The Alabamian was one of those who stayed to the bitter end, and put up a magnificent fight in the process. Despite falling morale, poor discipline and bad uniforms and equipment, those who did see it through have been called some of the best infantrymen ever to fight.

A contemporary woodcut of Confederate prisoners, an officer in the lead

Arms and Accoutrements

Besides his uniform, an English observer noted that each infantryman carried '. . . his musket and cartridge-box . . . a canteen, most men a blanket and haversack'. The cartridge-box was usually a copy of the U.S. cartridge-box, often of undyed brown leather. It was generally worn on the waistbelt, at the small of the back, held on by two straps. Inside, one or two tin containers held forty rounds or so of paper-wrapped ammunition. Some states issued brass stamped cartridge-box plates with a state pattern, such as its seal or letters

like 'NC' for North Carolina. These, however, were rare and most box flaps were plain or impressed 'CS'.

Finials on Union cartridge-boxes were always brass, but what brass there was in the Confederacy was needed for sabre hilts, cannon and musket parts. Confederates mostly used wood or lead finials.

'In action', recalled a veteran, 'the blanket roll is thrown further back, and the cartridge-box is drawn forward, frequently in front of the body'. Next to the cartridge-box was the cap-box. In it were held the small copper percussion caps used to fire the musket. Cap-boxes, too, were often brown with wood or lead finials, and held to the belt with one wide strap. Like the cartridge-box, they often lacked the second under-flap used as protection against rain in U.S. issue boxes.

In the centre of the belt was the belt-plate. This was most often just a plain brass frame buckle, with a single or double tongue. Some pre-war state-issue plates bore state seals or letters, like

Men in reconstructed Confederate uniforms give a good idea of a typical company in line of battle. The man on the far left is the company commander

'AVC' for Alabama Volunteer Corps or 'SC' for South Carolina. Many captured U.S. plates also saw use. The Confederate armouries did make some belt-plates, usually brass rectangles with the letters 'CSA' or oval brass plates with the letters 'CS'.

On the left hip the soldier was to wear his bayonet. Colonel Fremantle noted that among the soldiers 'Many, however, had lost or thrown away their bayonets, which they don't appear to value properly, as they assert that they have never met any Yankees who would wait for that weapon.' McCarthy agreed. 'The infantry found out that bayonets were not of much use, and did not hesitate to throw them, with the scabbard, away.'

Another veteran recalled: 'From the right shoulder pass two straps, one cloth the other leather, making a cross with the blanket roll on the breast and back. These straps support respectively a greasy cloth haversack and a flannel-covered canteen, captured from the Yankees. Added to the haversack strap is a tin cup while in addition to some odds and ends of camp trumpery, there hangs over his back a frying pan an invaluable utensil with which a soldier would be loath to part. His gun is an Enfield rifle, also captured from the enemy and substituted for the old flintlock musket or shotgun with which he was originally armed.'

The haversack, into which whatever rations he could lay his hands on, tobacco and any spare ammunition went, was usually made of white cotton duck or linen, although any sort of material would do. Captured Union ones were greatly prized.

Waterbottles, or canteens, were as varied in style as haversacks. Round tin Union ones, with wool covers, were commonly used, and a Confederate-made version of this canteen is usually marked by a tin, rather than pewter, spout.

Confederates also made tin drum-shaped canteens. Wood canteens, generally left the natural colour, were quite common. These were often carved with the owner's name and unit on one side. Leather and canvas were both used for slings.

The blanket roll was made up of a blanket brought from home or captured. Each soldier was supposed to have a shelter half and a waterproof – a poncho – as part of his blanket roll, but these were rare. After the Peninsular campaign Lee requested shelter halves, as the men were then sleeping under blankets thrown over rails during showers. At Fredericksburg, however, an issue of shelter halves was made to the men of the Light Division – at a ratio of one half for every twenty men.

The halves were made of heavy cotton duck with buttons and buttonholes on three sides. Two halves together made up a small tent for two men.

Waterproofs were to be made of indiarubber-coated muslin, with a slit in the middle through which the head went. General Josiah Gorgas, Chief of Confederate Ordnance, recalled an '. . . almost absolute lack of indiarubber, [so] extensive use was made of heavy cotton cloth, for some purposes in double or quadruple thicknesses heavily stitched together, treated with one or more coats of drying oil. Sheets of such cloth were issued to the men in the field for sleeping on damp ground, and belts, bridle reins and cartridge-boxes were made in whole or in part of the same material. Linseed oil answered best for making this cloth, and much was imported through the blockade, but it was eked out to some extent by fish oil. . . .'

Even if the infantryman had all he was supposed to have in his blanket roll, he never knew how long he would keep it. A private in the 17th Virginia, on the field going into the Second Battle of Manassas, recalled: 'On the way we were halted, and every soldier was compelled to strip for the fight by discarding his blanket – if he had one, which was not often – oilcloth or overcoat. All these were deposited in a large pile, and guards set over them, looking very much as if we did not intend to retreat. Cartridge-boxes were filled with forty rounds, and in our haversacks we carried twenty more, making sixty rounds in all.'

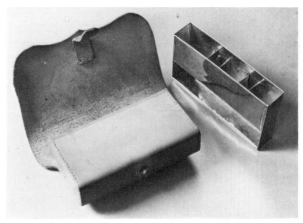

A cartridge-box said to be for the Austrian rifled musket and known to be Confederate-made. Ammunition was held in the tin container. (Author's collection)

It was when the infantryman was more interested in the final part of his kit – his musket – than anything else.

Infantrymen had been encouraged to bring arms from home at first, giving the army quite a variety of hunting rifles, flintlock muskets and shotguns. Arms-making machinery had been captured at Harper's Ferry, Virginia, in 1861, and sent to Richmond and Fayetteville, North Carolina, where armouries were immediately set up. Two-band rifles were turned out at Fayetteville, and three-band muskets at Richmond which, eventually, were as good as any Union make. These were, of course, close copies of the single-shot 0·58-calibre Model 1855 rifled muskets and rifles – excellent weapons, with an effective range of some 500 yards.

The 'classic' issue cap-box has a lead or wood finial, no under-flap and an impressed 'CS' on the flap. The brass frame buckle was the most commonly used. (Author's collection)

Agents were quickly sent overseas, too, and by 3 February 1863 had shipped back 70,980 long Enfield rifles, 9,715 short Enfield rifles, 354 Enfield carbines, 27,000 Austrian rifles, 21,040 British smoothbore muskets and 2,020 Brunswick rifles. Some 23,000 more muskets were awaiting shipment in London and 30,000 in Vienna. An officer of the Stonewall Brigade noted in January 1863 that 'during that time some Austrian rifles were distributed among the Second and Fifth (Virginia) Regiments'.

A problem with such a variety of weapons was that they had a variety of bore sizes, and ammunition resupply became a nightmare for quartermasters. Richmonds and captured U.S. muskets – the bulk of the army's weapons – were 0·58 calibre; Enfields were 0·577; old U.S. smoothbore muskets were 0·69, and Austrian muskets were 0·54. There were even some Prussian, Russian and Austrian 0·75-calibre muskets around. The British and American weapons were close enough to use the same ammunition, and it was eventually decided that the 0·577 calibre would be the official size.

By May 1863 pretty much the whole Army of Northern Virginia, through captures, homemakes or imports, had 0·577- or 0·58-calibre muskets. In fact, so many muskets were available that Colonel Fremantle was able to report that near Gordonsville, Virginia, '. . . I observed an enormous pile of excellent rifles rotting in the open air. These had been captured at Chancellorsville; but the Confederates have already such a superabundant stock of rifles that apparently they can afford to let them spoil.'

An Austrian bayonet and Confederate scabbard. (Author's collection)

Infantry

The Confederate infantryman in action was a different soldier from his enemy. One particular trait Fremantle noticed was that 'the Southern troops, when charging, or to express their delight always yell in a manner peculiar to themselves. The Yankee cheer is much more like ours; but the Confederate officers declare that the Rebel yell has a particular merit, and always produces a salutary and useful effect upon their adversaries. A corps is sometimes spoken of as a "good yelling regiment".'

While they might yell well, their drill was rather indifferent. Rarely did they learn all the facets of drill in their manual, which was written by their General Hardee when still in the U.S. Army. A British observer in 1861 said that 'the drill of the army is the same as the French, the step even quicker than the Zouaves, and a good deal longer than that of the English infantry. Movements are executed with considerable precision, and as rapidly as in English light-infantry battalions.'

Colonel Fremantle, during one review, '. . . expressed a desire to see them form square, but it appeared they were "not drilled to such a maneuver" (except square two deep). They said the country did not admit of cavalry charges, even if the Yankee cavalry had stomach to attempt it.'

Nor did their marching please Coldstreamer Fremantle. 'I saw no stragglers during the time I was with Pender's division; but although the Virginian army certainly does get over a deal of ground, yet they move at a slow, dragging pace, and are evidently not good marchers naturally. As Mr Norris [his Confederate guide] observed to me, "Before this war we were a lazy set of devils; our Negroes worked for us, and none of us ever dreamt of walking, though we all rode a great deal."'

Even more interesting were the men of Hood's Division. 'This division, well known for its fighting qualities, is composed of Texans, Alabamians, and Arkansians, and they certainly are a queer lot to look at. They carry less than any other troops;

Tin Confederate canteen. (Gettysburg National Military Park)

many of them have only got an old piece of carpet or rug as baggage; many have discarded their shoes in the mud; all are ragged and dirty, but full of good humour and confidence in themselves and their general, Hood.'

Artillery

Confederate artillerymen were even more self-confident, and with even less good reason. Many of them originally came from socially élite, pre-war units. Infantry companies were also converted into artillery batteries, as when Company 'A', 27th Volunteer Virginia Infantry, became the Allegheny Artillery, later Carpenter's Battery.

As the government set about making small-arms, it also began casting cannon, especially in Richmond and Macon, Georgia. Inferior metal, lack of facilities and few trained workmen made it difficult to make decent cannon, however. An ordnance officer reported in 1862 that 'many of these guns were defective and even dangerous. One battery from the Memphis foundry lost three guns in a month by bursting . . . [so] the finest cannons have been received from England. Several magnificent guns of the Whitworth and

Blakely patents I have seen or heard described as doing good execution among the "Yankees".'

Not many cannon nor much ammunition could be carried in crowded blockade-runners, and the Confederacy had to depend on itself – and captured U.S. supplies. Local arsenals made ammunition and fuses, although they were often faulty and would not explode at all or did so right at the muzzle.

Fremantle noted that 'the artillery horses are in poor condition, and get only 3 lb of corn [Indian corn] a day. The artillery is of all kinds – Parrots, Napoleons, rifled and smooth bores, all shapes and sizes. Most of them bear the letters U.S., showing that they have changed masters.'

The Parrot gun was a 10-lb rifled iron gun, with a large iron band placed on the gun's breech to reinforce it when fired. Confederates made a variation of it, but they were not commonly used. Colonel William Allen, Chief of Ordnance of II Corps, said later, 'We especially valued the three-inch rifles, which became the favorite field piece.' These were also iron 10-lb cannon, which were a U.S. issue.

According to Colonel Fremantle, however, Chief of Artillery General Pendelton disagreed with Colonel Allen. 'He said that the universal opinion is in favour of the 12-pounder Napoleon gun as the best and simplest sort of ordnance for field purposes. Nearly all the artillery with this army has been either captured from the enemy or cast from old 6-pounders taken at the early part of the war.'

The Napoleon, also a U.S.-issue weapon, was a

The average Confederate haversack was of duck, fastened with bone buttons. (Author's collection)

21

Men of Longstreet's Corps fire on a Federal supply train in a contemporary print

bronze smoothbore, which could fire solid shot, shrapnel or shell. It was widely made in the south.

For close work and in wooded areas, the smoothbore Napoleon, with a range of some 2,000 yards maximum and 1,619 yards at five degrees, was the superior weapon. At the same five degrees, however, the Parrot had a range of 1,900 yards and the three-inch rifle 1,830 yards – and both would hit accurately where the Napoleon would not. For real sharpshooting work, the army had a battery of 12-lb breech-loading Whitworth guns from England. At five degrees these had an accurate range of 2,750 yards.

Four guns made up the average Confederate battery. A captain would command it, and its designation was usually the captain's name, such as Crenshaw's Battery. Batteries formed in 1861 often named themselves after their area, as the Pee Dee Artillery, or an important person, as the Jeff Davis Artillery.

Each two guns made up a section, under a

lieutenant. Each gun, limber and caisson made up a 'piece' under the command of the chief of piece, a sergeant.

Lee felt his army had too much artillery, especially as it was difficult to feed all its horses. He left quite a number of batteries in Virginia on the first invasion of the North, ending at Sharpsburg, Maryland, in 1862. Upon his return, on 14 October 1862, he had fourteen batteries disbanded.

Artillery was not as effective in the Army of Northern Virginia as it could have been, due partly to its poor quality, but due equally to the policy of posting batteries to infantry brigades. As a result of that policy, Confederate guns were rarely used in any concentrated force. Therefore, the winter after Sharpsburg, batteries were taken from brigades and organized into battalions.

Each battalion was under a field officer, either a colonel or lieutenant-colonel, with an ordnance officer, quartermaster and an adjutant on its staff.

Each battalion commander reported to his corps' chief of artillery.

Despite the reorganization, artillery Colonel D. G. McIntosh wrote after the war that the artillery's '. . . use, generally, was fragmentary and detached, and nowhere did it achieve results comparable to the concentrated fire of the Union batteries at Malvern Hill'.

Artillerymen were to be armed with swords, and designs for Confederate swords were copied exactly from U.S. Army regulation ones. Southern-made ones were generally somewhat crude, their iron blades with unstopped blood gutters and reddish-brass, badly made hilts. Later made ones have, instead of leather grips, plain wood ones or ones wrapped in oilcloth. Mounts on sabre scabbards were often of brass, too, instead of iron.

Foot artillerymen were to carry short swords with wide blades. The idea was that the artillery-man whose gun was being overrun by cavalry would use this short sword to first disembowel his enemy's horse, then he would turn to the cavalry-man. Taking for granted, of course, the cavalry-man was doing nothing himself in the process.

Despite the fairly obvious lack of purpose in these swords, they were widely made, with hand-some 'CS' letters cast into all-brass hilts.

Wrote artilleryman McCarthy: 'The artillery-men, who started out with heavy sabers hanging to their belts, stuck them in the mud as they marched, and left them for the ordnance officers to pick up and turn over to the cavalry.'

Cavalry

Cavalry was at first thought to be the best of the Southern troops. Men in it brought their own horses – horses they had spent long years riding before the war. Added to their years of handling weapons while hunting, it was thought they would be magnificent cavalrymen.

A pro-Union observer in 1862 noted: 'So far as my observation extended, the Southern cavalry are superior to the loyal, for the kind of service expected of them. They are not relied upon for heavy charges against large bodies of infantry

Musket tools. Top row, from left, 0·58-calibre worm, sight wrench with screwdriver blades, 0·69-calibre worm. Bottom row, tumbler punches, spring vice, nipple wrench with screwdriver blades. (Author's collection)

closely massed, as in some of the wars of the Old World during the close of the last century and the first part of this; but for scouting, foraging, and sudden dashes against outposts and unguarded companies of their enemies. In this service, fleet-ness, perfect docility, and endurance for a few hours a day, are requisite in the make-up of the horses used. . . . And, then, with the exception of some of the Western troopers [of the U.S. Army], the Southerners are more perfect horsemen than our loyal cavalry. They have been on horseback, many of them, from youth, and are trained to the perfect control of themselves and their steeds in difficult circumstances. In addition to these causes of superiority, they have a basic advantage over the Federal troops in the present contest from two causes: It is hard to overestimate the advantage they find in a knowledge of the ground, the roads, the ravines, the hiding-places, the marshes, the fords, the forests, etc. But even more important than this is the sympathy they have from the inhabitants, almost universally, who give them information by every method, of the approach, strength, and plans of their enemies.'

Cavalrymen were armed with sabres, again often crude copies of the U.S.-issue cavalry sabres, pistols and carbines. The pistols were generally Confederate-made copies of the Colt 0·36-calibre,

Men in reconstructed Confederate dress demonstrate loading and shooting the rifled musket. They are, from left, aiming, reaching for a cartridge, and biting off the paper cartridge's end to expose the powder and pour it down the musket barrel

1 Corporal, 1st Virginia Regiment, 1861
2 Private, Charleston Zouave Cadets, 1861
3 Private, Louisiana Tigers, 1861

MICHAEL YOUENS

A

1 Private, 23rd Virginia Regiment, 1861
2 Cannoneer, Richmond Howitzers, 1861
3 Private, 1st Virginia Cavalry, 1861

1 First Lieutenant, 1st Texas Regiment, 1862
2 Private, 1st Florida Cavalry, 1862
3 Sergeant, 3rd South Carolina Regiment, 1862

MICHAEL YOUENS

C

1 Musician, 5th North Carolina Cavalry, 1862
2 Captain, Washington Artillery, 1862
3 Private, 8th Louisiana Regiment, 1862

D

1 Private, 14th Tennessee Regiment, 1862
2 Captain, 7th Georgia Cavalry, 1863
3 Cadet, Virginia Military Academy, 1863

MICHAEL YOUENS

E

1 Colonel, Haskell's Artillery Battalion, 1863
2 General Officer, 1863
3 Corporal, 1st Maryland Regiment, 1863

F

1 Chaplain, 4th Texas Regiment, 1863
2 Hospital Steward, 1863
3 General Officer, 1864

1 Private, 21st Mississippi Regiment, 1865
2 Major, 1st Regiment of C.S. Engineers, 1865
3 First Lieutenant, C.S. Marines, 1865

ix-shot revolver. Most of them were made with brass frames, instead of iron, and other cheaper materials were used where possible. They were, none the less, well-made weapons. Many cavalrymen carried two revolvers, if possible. Colonel Mosby's cavalrymen carried two revolvers on their waist-belts and two more in saddle holsters, with no sabres at all.

Men bringing weapons from home, instead of carbines, brought shotguns, and an amazing number of these saw use throughout the war. These were good enough for man-to-man engagements, but in a general mix-up the scattering shot was apt to hit friend and foe alike. Therefore, single-shot carbines were preferred.

The typical Confederate carbine was actually a muzzle-loading short version of the rifled musket, either a short Richmond or a copy of an Enfield. Such a weapon – loaded by tearing open a paper cartridge, pouring powder and ball down its muzzle, pulling out the ramrod and ramming the shot down, half cocking, flipping off the old cap and putting on a new one, and, finally, cocking to fire – was obviously inferior to U.S.-issue breech-loaders. Therefore the Richmond Armoury by spring 1863 began making copies of the 0·54-calibre Sharps breech-loading carbine.

Initial testing by the 4th Virginia Cavalry was unfavourable. According to a lieutenant in the regiment: 'Forty new Sharps rifles with Richmond stamp on them were handed yesterday to my company. The men were ordered to test them. Nine were fired, and seven of the nine burst.' Lee, himself, got into the act when he wrote Gorgas that the Richmond Sharps were '. . . so defective as to be demoralizing to our men'.

Actually, the Chief of Ordnance of the Cavalry Division reported the carbine to be '. . . an excellent weapon, but not perfectly put together'. However, the bad reputation had preceded the carbines, and unless they could obtain captured U.S. carbines, cavalrymen relied on the single-shot muzzle-loader throughout the war.

It was, too, that weapon the cavalrymen put their chief trust in. Wrote McCarthy: 'The cavalrymen found sabers very tiresome when hung to the belt, and adopted the plan of fastening them to the saddle on the left side, with the hilt in front and in reach of the hand. Finally sabers got very

The Confederates imported some 27,000 0·54-calibre Austrian rifled muskets. The lockplate on this one is dated 1861. (Author's collection)

scarce even among the cavalrymen, who relied more and more on their short rifles.'

Colonel Fremantle was surprised by Confederate cavalry being so unlike Regular cavalry: 'I remarked that it would be a good thing for them if on this occasion [at Gettysburg] they had cavalry to follow up the broken infantry in the event of their succeeding in beating them. But to my surprise they all spoke of their cavalry as not efficient for that purpose. In fact, Stuart's men, though excellent at making raids, capturing waggons and stores, and cutting off communications, seem to have no idea of charging infantry under any circumstances. Unlike the cavalry with Bragg's army, they wear swords, but seem to have little idea of using them – they hanker after their carbines and revolvers. They constantly ride with their swords between their left leg and the saddle, which has a very funny appearance; but their horses are generally good, and they ride well. The infantry and artillery of this army don't seem to respect the cavalry very much, and often jeer at them.'

There was, indeed, little respect for the cavalry from the other branches. General D. H. Hill was even said to offer a reward to anyone who could produce a dead cavalryman, killed in action with his spurs on. At this same Gettysburg campaign, an artillery colonel complained: 'Our cavalry did not give us the timely information, or the time to get ready, which was their chief duty. If Stuart, instead of being miles away, had been in position, guarding our advance, giving our infantry warning, engaging the enemy and masking our troops

A Confederate battery at Gettysburg is made up of a 12-lb Napoleon, foreground, and three-inch rifles, behind

killed. I heard his conduct on this occasion highly spoken of by all. Stuart's cavalry can hardly be called cavalry in the European sense of the word but, on the other hand, the country in which they are accustomed to operate is not adapted for cavalry.'

In fact, one real factor which discouraged cavalrymen from charging too gallantly was that if their horses were killed, they became infantrymen. An officer of Stuart's staff wrote: 'We now felt the bad effect of our system of requiring men to furnish their own horses. The most dashing trooper was the one whose horse was the most apt to get shot, and when this man was unable to remount himself he had to go to the infantry service and was lost to the cavalry. Such a penalty for gallantry was terribly demoralizing.'

Those remaining were in regiments composed of ten companies or squadrons of sixty to eighty privates, with a captain, a first lieutenant, two second lieutenants, five sergeants, four corporals, a farrier and a blacksmith. The regiment also included a colonel, a lieutenant-colonel, a major, an adjutant, a sergeant-major and a quartermaster-sergeant. Two to six regiments made up a brigade and as many as six brigades made up a division.

Horse artillery, ammunition and supply wagons and even rolling forges made up the rest of the Cavalry Corps.

until they all got together, there is every reason to think that we might have crushed the enemy in detail.'

Fremantle, as the rest of the army, was less than impressed on the whole with the cavalry. '. . . These cavalry fights are miserable affairs. Neither party has any idea of serious charging with the sabre. They approach one another with considerable boldness, until they get to within about forty yards, and then, at the very moment when a dash is necessary, and the sword alone should be used, they hesitate, halt, and commence a desultory fire with carbines and revolvers.

'An Englishman named Winthrop, a captain in the Confederate Army, and formerly an officer in H.M.'s 22nd regiment, although not in the cavalry himself, seized the colours of one of the [cavalry] regiments, and rode straight at the Yankees in the most gallant manner, shouting to the men to follow him. He continued to distinguish himself by leading charges until his horse was unfortunately

Technical and Medical Corps

A corps the other branches did respect was the Corps of Engineers.

In 1860 Virginia formed a state Corps of Engineers from the few professional engineers in the state to build a system of forts. This corps, made up of commissioned officers only, was merged into the Confederate Corps of Engineers when the government moved to Richmond.

During the Peninsular campaign, other ranks were needed to do fortification, road-building and bridge-construction work, and in June 1862 he Chief of Engineers of the Army of Northern Virginia was directed to take 300 men from each division to form a Corps of Pioneers to do this work. This Pioneer Corps did excellent work, although there were few of them and, because they were simply infantrymen, they were not well trained to do engineering work. An engineer officer, assigned to build a bridge near Richmond across the James River, could not get any Pioneers, and ended up having the Provost Marshal round up 500 men, marched under guard, to do the job. Civilians helped, too, on this job.

When the Army of the Potomac began really pushing the Army of Northern Virginia in late 1863, it was seen that regularily enlisted and trained engineers of all ranks were necessary. Therefore, two regiments, the 1st and 2nd Regiments of Confederate States Engineers, each to consist of ten companies of 100 men, were authorized by Congress.

According to a lieutenant-colonel of the 1st Engineers, the regiment was made up of '. . . men from twenty-five to thirty-five, mostly married, and skilled in the use of tools in some way or another, mechanics of all sorts, and farmers, etc. . . . The field and company officers were civil engineers by profession, also most of the lieutenants.'

Actually, their first time in the field, the engineers of the Army of Northern Virginia, which consisted of the 1st Regiment and two companies of the 2nd, served as infantry. Thereafter, they proved they could build fortifications and defend them with equal ease and ability. On the retreat to Appomattox the engineers were found in the van of the army, building bridges, and in the rear, holding off the enemy while destroying those bridges.

The other technical branch serving with the army was the Corps of Signallers, organized by E. P. Alexander, later Chief of Artillery. The corps did good work from the beginning. At the first battle of the war, First Manassas, they passed word on to the commanding general that Federal troops were moving on his left flank.

The corps was attached to the Adjutant-General's Department, and was responsible for signalling, the telegraph and all secret service work. In the field it did its work with flags during the day and torches at night. The telegraph could

A 'Stars and Bars' flag carried by a battery. (Smithsonian Institution)

be used at all times, in all weather, but a shortness of supplies of telegraph wire made the instrument a rarer one in the Confederate Army than in the Union Army.

The corps was also responsible for the Confederacy's one observation balloon, made from donated silk dresses of the ladies of the South. The balloon was filled with gas in Richmond, as no portable gas generators were available, and sent along the lines during the Peninsular campaign. One day the boat it was attached to ran aground and was captured – balloon and all. With it went perhaps the last silk dress in the Confederacy. Years later General Longstreet called its capture 'the meanest trick of the war' and said it was, of all things, the only thing he never forgave the Federal troops for.

Engineers and signallers wore white or buff facings when they simply didn't wear plain gray. Black, perhaps appropriately enough, was the facing colour worn by men of the Medical Department.

When the army was set up, a surgeon-general, equal in rank to a brigadier-general of cavalry, was appointed to head the entire department. He was to have 1,000 surgeons, each equal in rank to a cavalry major, and 2,000 assistant surgeons, each equal in rank to a cavalry captain. Their uniforms would be the same as regimental officers of their rank.

In addition, as many contract surgeons or acting assistant surgeons could be hired as needed, and they were equal to a second lieutenant of

A 12-lb Napoleon cannon

infantry. Later, all the acting assistant surgeons were examined by a medical board and either promoted to the rank of surgeon or assistant surgeon or dropped from the army's rolls.

Each regiment had a surgeon, an assistant surgeon and a hospital steward assigned to it. Each battalion and many artillery batteries were assigned an assistant surgeon.

At the brigade level the surgeon with the oldest commission was named senior surgeon of brigade. All the other surgeons were to report to him. At the same time, he was also responsible for his regimental duties. Most brigade staffs had an assistant surgeon appointed to them to handle the surgeon's paperwork.

The senior brigade surgeon was then named division surgeon, and received reports from all the other senior brigade surgeons. Each corps had a surgeon serving full-time on its staff as medical director.

Besides the regulation uniform, many surgeons wore green sashes. These were regulation in the U.S. Medical Department, and had come to represent an army medical man. In addition, wrote one surgeon, '. . . on the front of the cap or hat were the letters "M.S." embroidered in gold embraced by two olive branches'. Although Confederates rarely wore cap badges, this badge seems to have been used. One assistant surgeon in 186? wrote that he '. . . appeared in the dress of an assistant-surgeon, with the M.S. on my cap . . .'.

While many doctors in gray were excellent indeed, many more were rather poorly qualified for their jobs. One obtained his commission as an assistant surgeon on the grounds that '. . . as I had, while at School in New York, frequented the hospitals, and also attended two courses of medical lectures, I had gained a little knowledge of wounds and their treatment. This fact, and a special fondness, if not aptitude, for that study, decided my future course', i.e. of being an assistant surgeon.

Despite his own lack of great qualifications, he did find some practices to criticize in the Medical Department: 'While the surgeons, as a body, did their duty nobly, there were some young men, apparently just out of college, who performed difficult operations with the assurance and assumed skill of practiced surgeons, and with little regard for human life or limb.'

Considering the work set out for the surgeon, who was usually supplied with few drugs, it is probably just as well he had that self-assurance.

In action, the regimental surgeon set up a field hospital, while the assistant surgeon followed the regiment into action. The hospital steward either stayed to assist the surgeon or went with the assistant surgeon.

The hospital steward was often a medical student. His was a non-commissioned rank, equal to that of the orderly sergeant. Indeed, his stripes were the three chevrons and diamond of the orderly sergeant. He was in charge of the medicines, and made sure each man received what was prescribed for him. He was also present at sick call each morning.

The hospital steward was also in charge of the infirmary detail, although the assistant surgeon led that in combat.

The infirmary detail was initially made up of

Confederate regiments charge to defeat at Malvern Hill in this contemporary print

the regimental band and went into action behind the regiment. Each man carried a knapsack with dressings, stimulants, tourniquets and other first-aid equipment, and every two men carried a stretcher. They, under the eye of the assistant surgeon, were to patch up the wounded and bring them back to the field hospital for treatment.

If the wound was major, and with the soft 0·58-calibre bullets most wounds were major, the man would be sent back for further treatment and, hopefully, to recover. Most men in the Army of Northern Virginia ended up at the giant Chimborazo Hospital in Richmond, where some 76,000 patients were treated during the war. The hospital could handle some 4,800 men at one time in its 150 one-storey buildings. It had a bakery which could turn out 10,000 loaves of bread daily, an ice-house, soup kitchens, and a farm of 200 cows and almost as many goats.

Later regimental bands grew scarce and were relieved of infirmary detail work. During the Battle of Gettysburg Fremantle recalled: 'When the cannonade was at its height, a Confederate band of music, between the cemetery and our-selves, began to play polkas and waltzes, which sounded very curious, accompanied by the hissing and bursting of the shells.'

By then convalescents were assigned to the infirmary detail, although they were as little trained for that work as the bandsmen, and prob-ably less. They were, however, set aside as men specifically and constantly in the Infirmary Corps. Fremantle noted: 'In the rear of each regiment were from twenty to thirty Negro slaves, and a certain number of unarmed men carrying stret-chers and wearing in their hats the red badge of the Ambulance Corps; this is an excellent institution, for it prevents unwounded men falling out on pretence of taking wounded to the rear.' Later, as the men from the ill-fated Pickett's charge were returning to their lines, Fremantle '. . . began to meet many wounded men returning from the

An artillery captain's coat. (Smithsonian Institution)

front. Many of them asked in piteous tones the way to a doctor or an ambulance. The further I got, the greater became the number of the wounded. At last I got to a perfect stream of them flocking through the woods in numbers as great as the crowd in Oxford Street in the middle of the day. Some were walking alone on crutches composed of two rifles, others were supported by men less badly wounded than themselves, and others were carried on stretchers by the Ambulance Corps; but in no case did I see a sound man helping the wounded to the rear, unless he carried the red badge of the Ambulance Corps.'

Discipline within the Infirmary Corps and helping the wounded seems to have been one of the bright spots in the Confederate discipline picture. A lieutenant-colonel in Gregg's Brigade at Second Manassas recalled that '. . . it was one of the

cruelties of our position, that before the Infirmary Corps were allowed to help a wounded man before his wound was looked at, he must be stripped of his accoutrements, and his ammunition distributed among his comrades.'

Command

As an Infirmary Corps, not originally planned but seen to be necessary, was organized, so the entire army as the needs arose organized itself. Under the original plan the highest command possible was a division, commanded by a major-general. It was quickly seen that an army of a large number of divisions as the largest bodies of men under a single commander was an army difficult to control. Therefore, Lee set up informal 'commands', one of which was held by Longstreet and one by Jackson, each made up of several divisions. General John Magruder at first held one of the commands, but was transferred west.

On 8 September 1862 the 'commands' were formalized into corps by legislation passed by Congress, and the corps commanders were named lieutenant-generals. Lee became a full general.

These commanders, and mostly Lee, held the army together by pure personal power and abilities when arms and equipment were few, morale and discipline was bad, and future prospects were dim. Lord Wolseley, visiting the army in August 1862 reported: 'The feeling of the soldiers for General Lee resembles that which Wellington's troops entertained for him – namely, a fixed and unshakeable faith in all he did, and a calm confidence of victory when serving under him. But Jackson, like Napoleon, is idolized with that intense fervour which, consisting of mingled personal attachment and devoted loyalty, causes them to meet death for his sake, and bless him when dying.'

The death of Jackson, in many ways, caused this love to be transferred to Lee, the brightest star among a constellation of bright Confederate military stars. And this love continued until, and after, the issuance of the Army of Northern Virginia's General Order Number Nine:

'After four years of arduous service marked by

The 1st Virginia Cavalry, an élite regiment, rests during a march in a contemporary print

unsurpassed courage and fortitude the Army of Northern Virginia has been compelled to yield to overwhelming numbers and resources.

'I need not tell the survivors of so many hard-fought battles who have remained steadfast to the last that I have consented to this result from no distrust of them.

'But feeling that valour and devotion could accomplish nothing that could compensate for the loss that would have attended the continuance of the contest I have determined to avoid the useless sacrifice of those whose past services have endeared them to their country.

'By the terms of the agreement officers and men can return to their homes and remain until exchanged. You will take with you the satisfaction that proceeds from the consciousness of duty faithfully performed, and I earnestly pray that a merciful God will extend to you his blessing and protection. With an unceasing admiration of your constancy and devotion to your country

and a grateful remembrance of your kind and generous consideration for myself, I bid you an affectionate farewell.

R E Lee/Genl

Hd. Qrs. Army Northern Virginia/April 10th 1865'

MAJOR ACTIONS OF THE ARMY OF NORTHERN VIRGINIA*

1862

The Seven Days, 26 June–1 July: Jackson's Command, Magruder's Command
Second Manassas, Va., 30 August: Longstreet's Command, Jackson's Command
Sharpsburg, Md., 17 Sept.: Longstreet's Command, Jackson's Command

* Confederate battle designations sometimes differ from Union ones, and the Confederate designation is given here.

John S. Mosby, leader of a Virginia cavalry battalion, wears a semi-military waistcoat and a single-breasted frock-coat with the single star of a major on each collar

J. E. B. Stuart, commander of the Cavalry Corps, wears his coat lapels buttoned over. His buff sash is regulation for a general officer

Fredericksburg, Va., 13 Dec.: Longstreet's Corps, Jackson's Corps, Cavalry Corps

1863

Chancellorsville, Va., 1–4 May: McLaw's, Anderson's Divs., Longstreet's Corps, Jackson's Corps, Cavalry Corps
Beverly Ford and Brandy Station, Va., 9 June: Cavalry Corps
Gettysburg, Pa., 1–3 July: Longstreet's Corps, Ewell's Corps, Hill's Corps, Cavalry Corps
Mine Run, Va., 26–28 Nov.: Longstreet's Corps, Ewell's Corps, Hill's Corps

1864

Wilderness, Va., 5–7 May: Longstreet's Corps, Ewell's Corps, Hill's Corps, Cavalry Corps
Cold Harbor, Va., 1 June: Longstreet's Corps, Ewell's Corps, Hill's Corps, Cavalry Corps
Cedar Creek, Va., 19 Oct.: Ramseur's Div., Pegram's Div., Gordon's Div., Kershaw's Div., Wharton's Div., Lomax's (Cavalry) Div., Rosser's (Cavalry) Div., Artillery
Siege of Petersburg, Va., 15 June on: Longstreet's

Corps, Gordon's Corps, Hill's Corps, Cavalry Corps

1865

Appomattox Campaign, 1–9 April: Longstreet's Corps, Gordon's Corps, Hill's Corps, Anderson's Corps, Cavalry Corps, G. W. C. Lee's Div.

ORGANIZATION OF THE ARMY OF NORTHERN VIRGINIA AS OF JUNE 1862

JACKSON'S COMMAND
Whiting's Division. Hood's Brigade: 18th Ga., 1st Tex., 4th Tex., 5th Tex. Law's Brigade: 4th Ala., 2nd Miss., 11th Miss., 6th N.C. Artillery: Staunton Arty., Rowan Arty.
Jackson's Division. Winder's (Stonewall) Brigade: 2nd Va., 4th Va., 5th Va., 27th Va., 33rd Va., Allegheny Arty., Rockbridge Arty. Cunningham's Brigade: 21st Va., 42nd Va., 48th Va., 1st Va. (Irish) Battn., Hampden Arty. Fulkerson's Brigade: 10th Va., 23rd Va., 37th Va., Danville

Arty. Lawton's Brigade: 13th Ga., 26th Va., 31st Ga., 38th Ga., 60th Ga., 61st Ga.

Ewell's Division. Elzey's Brigade: 12th Ga., 13th Va., 25th Va., 31st Va., 44th Va., 52nd Va., 58th Va. Trimble's Brigade: 15th Ala., 21st Ga., 16th Miss., 21st N.C., 1st N.C. Battn. Sharpshooters, Courtney's Battery. Taylor's Brigade: 6th La., 7th La., 8th La., 9th La., 1st La. Special Battn., Charlottesville Arty. Maryland Line: 1st Inf., Co. 'A' Md. Cav., Balto. Battery.

Hill's Division. Rhodes's Brigade: 3rd Ala., 5th Ala., 6th Ala., 12th Ala., 26th Ala., King William Arty. Anderson's Brigade: 2nd N.C., 4th N.C., 14th N.C., 30th N.C., Hardaway's Battery. Garland's Brigade: 5th N.C., 12th N.C., 13th N.C., 20th N.C., 23rd N.C., Jeff Davis Arty. Colquitt's Brigade: 13th Ala., 6th Ga., 23rd Ga., 27th Ga., 28th Ga. Ripley's Brigade: 44th Ga., 48th Ga., 1st N.C., 3rd N.C. Artillery: Hanover Arty.

MAGRUDER'S COMMAND

Jones's Division. Toombs's Brigade: 2nd Ga., 15th Ga., 17th Ga., 20th Ga. Anderson's Brigade: 1st Ga. (Regulars), 7th Ga., 8th Ga., 9th Ga., 11th

A typical pair of officer's field-glasses, made in France. (Author's collection)

Ga. Artillery: Wise Arty, Washington Arty, Madison Arty, Dabney's Battery.

McLaw's Division. Semmes's Brigade: 10th Ga., 53rd Ga., 5th La., 10th La., 15th Va., 32nd Va. Kershaw's Brigade: 2nd S.C., 3rd S.C., 7th S.C., 8th S.C., Alexandria Arty.

Magruder's Division. Cobb's Brigade: 16th Ga., 24th Ga., Ga. Legion (Cobb's), 2nd La., 15th N.C., Troup Arty. Barksdale's Brigade: 13th Miss., 17th Miss., 18th Miss., 21st Miss., 1st Richmond Howitzers. Artillery: Pulaski Arty., James City Arty., Magruder Arty.

Longstreet's Division. Kemper's Brigade: 1st Va., 7th Va., 11th Va., 17th Va., 24th Va., Loudoun Arty. Anderson's Brigade: 2nd S.C. (Rifles), 4th S.C. Battn., 5th S.C., 6th S.C., Palmetto (S.C.) Sharpshooters. Pickett's Brigade: 8th Va., 18th Va., 19th Va., 28th Va., 56th Va. Wilcox's Brigade: 8th Ala., 9th Ala., 10th Ala., 11th Ala., Thomas Arty. Pryor's Brigade: 14th Ala., 2nd Fal., 14th Va., 1st La. Battn., 3rd Va., Donaldsonville Arty. Featherston's Brigade: 12th Miss., 19th Miss., 2nd Miss. Battn., 3rd Richmond Howitzers. Artillery: Washington Arty., Lynchburg Arty., Dixie Arty.

Huger's Division. Mahone's Brigade: 6th Va., 12th Va., 16th Va., 41st Va., 49th Va., Portsmouth Arty. Wright's Brigade: 44th Ala., 3rd Ga., 4th Ga., 22nd Ga., 1st La., Huger's Battery. Armistead's Brigade: 9th Va., 14th Va., 38th Va., 53rd Va., 57th Va., 5th Va. Battn., Fauquier Arty., Turner's Battery.

Hill's (Light) Division. Field's Brigade: 40th Va., 47th Va., 55th Va., 60th Va. Gregg's Brigade: 1st S.C., 1st S.C. Rifles, 12th S.C., 13th S.C., 14th S.C. Anderson's Brigade: 14th Ga., 35th Ga., 45th Ga., 49th Ga., 3rd La. Battn. O'Branch's Brigade: 7th N.C., 18th N.C., 28th N.C., 33rd N.C., 37th N.C. Archer's Brigade: 5th Ala. Battn., 19th Ga., 1st Tenn., 7th Tenn., 14th Tenn. Pender's Brigade: 2nd Ark. Battn., 16th N.C., 22nd N.C., 34th N.C., 38th N.C., 22nd Va. Battn. Artillery: Snowden Andrews's Battery, German Arty., Fredericksburg Arty., Crenshaw's Battery, Letcher Arty., Johnson's Battery, Masters's Battery, Pee Dee Arty., Purcell Arty.

Holmes's Division. Ramson's Brigade: 24th N.C., 25th N.C., 26th N.C., 35th N.C., 48th N.C., 49th N.C. Daniel's Brigade: 43rd N.C., 45th N.C.,

The Confederates' best supplier was the Federal government. Confederate cavalrymen 'draw' new supplies from a just-captured U.S. supply train

50th N.C., Burroughs's Cavalry Battn. Walker's Brigade: 3rd Ark., 2nd Ga. Battn., 27th N.C., 46th N.C., 30th Va., Goodwyn's Cavalry Co. Artillery: Branch's Battery, Brem's Battery, French's Battery, Graham's Battery.

WISE'S COMMAND
26th Va., 46th Va., Andrews's Battery, Rives's Battery.

RESERVE ARTILLERY
1st Va. Arty., Williamsburg Arty., Richmond Fayette Arty., Watson's Battery. Jones's Battalion: Clark's Battery, Orange Arty., Rhett's Battery. 1st Battn. (Sumpter) Arty.: Blackshear's Battery, Lane's Battery, Price's Battery, Ross's Battery, Hamilton's (Regular) Battery. Second Battn.: Fluvanna Arty., Milledge's Battery, Ashland Arty. Third Battn.: Fluvanna Arty., Amherst Arty., Morris Arty.

CAVALRY
1st N.C., 1st Va., 4th Va., 5th Va., 9th Va., 10th Va., Ga. Legion, 15th Va. Battn., Hampton Legion, Jeff Davis Legion, Stuart's Horse Arty.

ORGANIZATION OF THE ARMY OF NORTHERN VIRGINIA AS OF APRIL, 1865

H.Q. Escort: 39th Va. Battn. *Provost Guard:* 1st Va. Battn., Co. 'B' 44th Va. Battn. *Engineers:* 1st Regt., two companies, 2nd Regt.

LONGSTREET'S CORPS
Pickett's Division. Steuart's Brigade: 9th Va., 14th Va., 38th Va., 53rd Va., 57th Va. Corse's Brigade: 15th Va., 17th Va., 29th Va., 30th Va., 32nd Va. Hunton's Brigade: 8th Va., 18th Va., 19th Va., 28th Va., 56th Va. Terry's Brigade: 1st Va., 3rd Va., 7th Va., 11th Va., 24th Va.
Field's Division. Perry's (late Law's) Brigade: 4th Ala., 15th Ala., 44th Ala., 47th Ala., 48th Ala. Anderson's Brigade: 7th Ga., 8th Ga., 9th Ga.,

11th Ga., 59th Ga. Benning's Brigade: 2nd Ga., 15th Ga., 17th Ga., 20th Ga., Bratton's Brigade: 1st S.C., 5th S.C., 6th S.C., 2nd S.C. (Rifles), Palmetto (S.C.) Sharpshooters. Gregg's Brigade: 3rd Ark., 1st Tex., 4th Tex., 5th Tex.

Kershaw's Division. Du Bose's Brigade: 16th Ga., 18th Ga., 24th Ga., 3rd Ga. Battn. Sharpshooters, Cobb's Ga. Legion, Phillips's Ga. Legion. Humphrey's Brigade: 13th Miss., 17th Miss., 18th Miss., 21st Miss. Simms's Brigade: 10th Ga., 50th Ga., 51st Ga., 53rd Ga.

Artillery: Haskell's Battn.: Flanner's Battery, Ramsey's Battery, Garden's Battery, Lamkin's Battery. Huger's Battn.: Moody's Battery, Fickling's Battery, Parker's Battery, Smith's Battery, Taylor's Battery, Woolfolk's Battery.

GORDON'S CORPS

Grimes' (late Rhodes') Division. Battle's Brigade: 3rd Ala., 5th Ala., 6th Ala., 12th Ala., 61st Ala. Grimes's Brigade: 32nd N.C., 43rd N.C., 45th N.C., 53rd N.C., 2nd N.C. Battn. Cox's Brigade: 1st N.C., 2nd N.C., 3rd N.C., 4th N.C., 14th N.C., 30th N.C. Cook's Brigade: 4th Ga., 12th Ga., 21st Ga., 44th Ga., Patterson's Battery. Archer's Battn.: 3rd Battn. of Va. Reserves, 44th Battn. of Va. Reserves.

Early's Division. Johnston's Brigade: 5th N.C., 12th N.C., 20th N.C., 23rd N.C., 1st N.C. Battn. Lewis's Brigade: 6th N.C., 21st N.C., 54th N.C., 57th N.C. Walker's (late Pegram's) Brigade: 13th Va., 31st Va., 49th Va., 52nd Va., 58th Va.

Gordon's Division. Evans's Brigade: 13th Ga., 26th Ga., 31st Ga., 38th Ga., 60th and 61st Ga. (combined), 9th Ga. Battn. Arty., 18th Ga. Battn. Arty. Terry's Brigade: 2nd Va., 4th Va., 5th Va., 10th Va., 21st Va., 23rd Va., 25th Va., 27th Va., 33rd Va., 37th Va., 42nd Va., 44th Va. York's Brigade: 1st La., 2nd La., 5th La., 6th La., 7th La., 8th La., 9th La., 10th La., 14th La., 15th La.

Artillery: Braxton's Battn.: Carpenter's Battery, Cooper's Battery, Hardwicke's Battery. Cutshaw's Battn.: Reese's Battery, Carter's Battery, Montgomery's Battery, Fry's Battery, Garber's Battery, Jones's Battery. Hardaway's Battn.: Dance's Battery, Graham's Battery, Griffin's Battery, Smith's Battery. Johnson's Battn.: Clutter's Battery, Pollock's Battery. Lightfoot's Battn.: Caroline Arty., Nelson Arty., Surry Arty. Stark's Battn.:

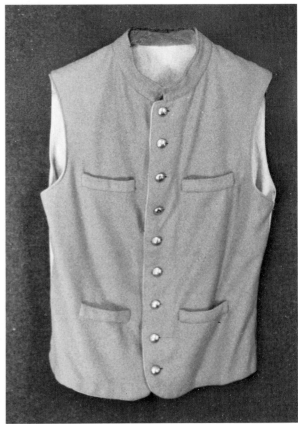

Confederate butternut wool officer's vest. (Author's collection)

Green's Battery, French's Battery, Armistead's Battery.

HILL'S CORPS *Provost Guard:* 5th Ala. Battn.

Heth's Division. Davis's Brigade: 1st Confederate Battn., 2nd Miss., 11th Miss., 26th Miss., 42nd Miss. Cooke's Brigade: 15th N.C., 27th N.C., 46th N.C., 48th N.C., 55th N.C. MacRae's Brigade: 11th N.C., 26th N.C., 44th N.C., 47th N.C., 52nd N.C. McComb's Brigade: 2nd Md. Battn., 1st Tenn. (Provisional Army), 7th Tenn., 14th Tenn., 17th and 23rd Tenn. (combined), 25th and 44th Tenn. (combined), 63rd Tenn.

Wilcox's Division. Thomas's Brigade: 14th Ga., 35th Ga., 45th Ga., 49th Ga. Lane's Brigade: 18th N.C., 28th N.C., 33rd N.C., 37th N.C., McGowan's Brigade: 1st S.C. (Provisional Army), 12th S.C., 13th S.C., 14th S.C., Orr's S.C. Rifles. Scales's Brigade: 13th N.C., 16th N.C., 22nd N.C., 34th N.C., 38th N.C.

Mahone's Division. Forney's Brigade: 8th Ala., 9th Ala., 10th Ala., 11th Ala., 13th Ala., 14th Ala.

General Robert E. Lee, centre, greets his defeated troops after Pickett's charge at Gettysburg in this diorama at Gettysburg National Military Park

Weisiger's Brigade: 6th Va., 12th Va., 16th Va., 41st Va., 61st Va. Harris's Brigade: 12th Miss., 16th Miss., 19th Miss., 48th Miss. Sorrel's Brigade: 3rd Ga., 22nd Ga., 48th Ga., 64th Ga., 2nd Ga. Battn., 10th Ga. Battn. Finegan's Brigade: 2nd Fla., 5th Fla., 8th Fla., 9th Fla., 10th Fla., 11th Fla.
Artillery. McIntosh's Battn.: Hurt's Battery, Chamberlayne's Battery, Price's Battery, Donald's Battery. Poague's Battn.: Richards's Battery, Williams's Battery, Johnston's Battery, Utterback's Battery, Perrick's Battery., 13th Va. Battn.: Otey's Battery, Ringgold Battery. Richardson's Battn.: Gregg's Battery, Cayce's Battery, Ellett's Battery, Brander's Battery.

ANDERSON'S CORPS

Johnson's Division. Wise's Brigade: 26th Va., 34th Va., 46th Va., 59th Va. Wallace's Brigade: 17th S.C., 18th S.C., 22nd S.C., 23rd S.C., 26th S.C., Holcombe S.C. Legion. Moody's Brigade: 41st Ala., 43rd Ala., 59th Ala., 60th Ala., 23rd Ala. Battn. Ransom's Brigade: 24th N.C., 25th N.C., 35th N.C., 49th N.C., 56th N.C.
Artillery. Blount's Battn.: Slaten's Battery, Cumming's Battery, Miller's Battery, Young's Battery.

Coit's Battn.: Bradford's Battery, R. G. Pegram's Battery, Wright's Battery. Stribling's Battn.: Dickerson's Battery, Marshall's Battery, Macon's Battery, Sullivan's Battery. Smith's Battn.: 1st Md. Arty., Johnston's Battery, Neblett's Battery, Drewry's Battery, Kevill's Battery.

CAVALRY CORPS

Fitzhugh Lee's Division. Munford's Brigade: 1st Va., 2nd Va., 3rd Va., 4th Va. Payne's Brigade: 5th Va., 6th Va., 8th Va., 36th Va. Battn. Gary's Brigade: 7th Ga., 7th S.C., Hampton's S.C. Legion, 24th Va.
W. H. F. Lee's Division. Barringer's Brigade: 1st N.C., 2nd N.C., 3rd N.C., 5th N.C. Beale's Brigade: 9th Va., 10th Va., 13th Va., 14th Va. Roberts's Brigade: 4th N.C., 16th N.C. Battn.
Rosser's Division. Dearing's Brigade: 7th Va., 11th Va., 12th Va., 35th Va. Battn. McCausland's Brigade: 16th Va., 17th Va., 21st Va., 22nd Va.
Artillery. Chew's Battn.: Graham's Battery, McGregor's Battery. Breathed's Battn.: P. P. Johnston's Battery, Shoemaker's Battery, Thompson's Battery.
G. W. C. Lee's Division. (Composed of Barton's and Crutchfield's Brigades, with Tucker's Naval Battalion attached.)

SELECT BIBLIOGRAPHY

Albaugh, William A., and Simmons, Edward, *Confederate Arms*, Harrisburg, 1958.
Fremantle, Lieutenant-Colonel A.J.L., *The Fremantle Diary*, New York, 1954.
Lord, Francis, *Civil War Collector's Encyclopedia*, Harrisburg, 1963.
Miller, F., *Photographic History of the Civil War*, New York, 1909.
McCarthy, Francis, *Detailed Minutiae of Soldier Life in the Army of Northern Virginia*, Richmond, 1882.
Wiley, Bell I., *The Life of Johnny Reb*, Indianapolis, Indiana, 1943.

The Plates

A1 Corporal, 1st Virginia Regiment, 1861

The 1st Virginia, recruited round Richmond, was made up of many of the best local families. Each company had a slightly different dress, although gray was the common colour. This corporal, marked by his chevrons, is a member of Company 'F', which copied the uniforms of two other companies, the Richmond Grays and the Montgomery Guard.

A2 Private, Charleston Zouave Cadets, 1861

The Zouave Cadets were a company of the 1st South Carolina Regiment of Rifles, raised in Charleston. The uniform illustrated is the summer one, while in winter the company wore a uniform of the 'full chasseur type, gray with red collar, cuffs, and lace and russet leather *zouave* leggings'.

A3 Private, Louisiana Tigers, 1861

The regiment was raised in New Orleans, mostly of Irishmen. They were issued brown *zouave* jackets with red trim, but often fought in their shirtsleeves. Instead of their fezzes, they often wore wide-brimmed straw hats, usually with a motto round the band, e.g. 'Tiger Looking For Old Abe'. Their trousers are said to have been made of bed-ticking.

B1 Private, 23rd Virginia Regiment, 1861

The Brooklyn Grays, organized in Brooklyn, Halifax County, in March 1861, were Company 'E', 23rd Virginia. Their belts were of white webbing instead of leather – the state issued 57,912 yards of the material to its troops in 1861. By August 1861 many of the men switched to short jackets; however, an original coat worn by a first sergeant in the regiment still exists, and it is the full-length frock-coat with black chevrons and no other trim. Its owner was killed in 1863.

B2 Cannoneer, Richmond Howitzers, 1861

The 1st Virginia had an artillery company, the Richmond Howitzers, when it was first organized.

Uniforms and regimental colour of the 1st Maryland Infantry were authentically re-created by this group at the re-enactment of First Manassas in 1961

The Howitzers shortly afterwards were made a separate battery, however. On 30 November 1860 the company was ordered to meet in 'fatigue dress, overcoats, with sabres and white gloves'. The men also had frock-coats with wings, which they obtained in October 1860.

B3 Private, 1st Virginia Cavalry, 1861

The men of the 1st Virginia Cavalry, under Colonel J. E. B. Stuart's, considered themselves in an élite unit. Most of them had ridden since childhood and were used to good horses and hard riding. They provided their own horses and firearms. The officers had yellow collars and cuffs, although many of the men had all-black trim. The wide strap across the man's body holds his carbine, a single-shot, muzzle-loading weapon.

C1 First Lieutenant, 1st Texas Regiment, 1862

For some time after the official dress regulations came out many officers continued to wear U.S. Army shoulder-straps. This lieutenant wears the star badge of Texas on his slouch hat and belt-plate. His standing coat collar has been turned down so that his tie and shirt collar show. Ties were rarely worn in the field.

C2 Private, 1st Florida Cavalry, 1862

A cavalry colonel serving in western Virginia reported to the War Department on 8 October

Monument to Virginia's troops at Gettysburg

1861 that 'I can but regret the necessity which deprives the officers and men of my command of the weapons adapted to a cavalry charge, and which they have shown themselves so well qualified to make daring and effective use of, especially so when they are opposed to an enemy well equipped in all these particulars, and whom if they meet in a hand-to-hand conflict they must oppose with clubbed rifles and shot-guns against revolvers and sabers.' This Floridian, taken from an original photograph, carries only a shotgun, probably brought from home.

C3 Sergeant, 3rd South Carolina Regiment, 1862
The 3rd South Carolina was organized in 1861 and wore uniforms donated by its home towns – uniforms not generally replaced until the autumn of 1863. The sergeant has managed to acquire a regulation *képi*, and his coat with sky-blue facings is more regulation than most of his regiment probably wears. His musket is a British Enfield. He carries an issue waterproof, made of oil-treated cotton, round his blanket.

D1 Musician, 5th North Carolina Cavalry, 1862
Confederate musicians were not marked with any special lace or badges. By luck, this musician has acquired a totally regulation cavalry musician's uniform. His trousers are captured U.S. cavalry-man's, much preferred because their seats are reinforced so as not to wear out quickly when riding. Sky-blue trousers were virtually never made in the Confederacy, although officially they were the regulation colour.

D2 Captain, Washington Artillery, 1862
The Washington Artillery was organized in 1838 and was known for its Mexican-American War service. The original uniforms were dark blue, although as they wore out they were replaced by gray. The captain, who wears his original issue coat, has U.S. Army shoulder-straps as his rank insignia. The silk sash, worn across the body, marks him as the 'officer of the day'. At all other times the sash was worn round the waist. The officer's trousers were originally to be sky-blue, but all colours were worn in service.

D3 Private, 8th Louisiana Regiment, 1862

The all-gray uniform became fairly standard Confederate dress by 1862, although shades of gray differed greatly from man to man. Most uniforms were made at home for individual soldiers with whatever materials could be locally obtained. This man also has a bit of trim on his cuffs, although this was not uniform for the whole regiment. Most men in the 8th were Creoles and few could speak any English.

E1 Private, 14th Tennessee Regiment, 1862

In the rush to arm men even old flintlock muskets, going as far back as the American War of 1812, were hauled out and given to the men – especially in rural states like Tennessee. The 14th served about this time in western Virginia, where a Union officer reported on 16 November 1861: 'I met one boy with a flint-lock rifle and a Confederate uniform. He acknowledged to have been in the Confederate service. . . .' As this man has no bayonet, he has provided himself with a knife.

E2 Captain, 7th Georgia Cavalry, 1863

Other than his all-gray cap and trousers, this captain has a regulation kit. Gray, rather than the regulation colours, was most common for trousers and caps. His men, however, are more apt to be clothed in light brown trousers, jackets and old slouch hats. The captain's belt-plate has his state seal on it.

E3 Cadet, Virginia Military Academy, 1863

Stonewall Jackson had been a professor at V.M.I. in 1861 and many leading officers had been graduated from the Academy then as now. The Cadet Corps itself participated in the Battle of New Market in 1864. One cadet wrote later: 'In May, 1862, the cadets had been marched to Jackson's aid at McDowell in the Shenandoah Valley. They had arrived too late to take part in the battle, but the effect of the march had been to wear out the last vestige of the peace uniforms. Then we had resort to coarse sheep's gray jackets and trousers, with seven buttons, and a plain black tape stripe. . . . We were content with a simple forage cap, blue or gray, as we could procure it . . . we had a plain leather cartridge-box, and a waist-belt with a harness buckle . . . we went

A three-inch rifle

into the battle of New Market with muzzle-loading Belgian rifles as clumsy as pickaxes.

'As the war progressed, our uniforms ceased to be uniforms; for as the difficulty of procuring cloth increased we were permitted to supply ourselves with whatever our parents could procure, and in time we appeared in every shade from Melton gray to Georgia butternut.'

F1 Colonel, Haskell's Artillery Battalion, 1863

Colonel J. C. Haskell, who lost an arm early in the war, recovered to command a battalion through many important battles and surrendered at Appomattox. His uniform, taken from a period photograph of himself, was quite close to the regulation one.

F2 General Officer, 1863

Generals took some liberties with their dress. This one, based on Major-General J. B. Gordon's photograph, has eliminated his regulation Austrian knot on the sleeves, and his collar is gray with a white oval badge with his rank insignia embroidered on it. His belt-plate is the U.S. officer's type.

F3 Corporal, 1st Maryland Regiment, 1863

The 1st Maryland began the war in *képis*, but, as most Confederates, later switched to slouch hats. The mark of a Marylander was the black Calvert cross sewn on the soldier's left breast. His blanket was sent from home as, in fact, many supplies for Marylanders were.

G1 Chaplain, 4th Texas Regiment, 1863

A minister in Richmond wrote the editor of the *Richmond Enquirer* on 25 September 1861, that 'I observed a Chaplain (Rev. Nicholas A. Davis, of Texas) in uniform yesterday, which uniform I admired above anything I have yet seen. A suit of black clothing strait breasted, with one row of brass buttons, and simple pointed cuff with a small *olive branch* about six inches long, running up the sleeve. . . . No stripes on the pants.' Davis was chaplain of the 4th Texas. Chaplains were to supply their own dress and seem to have had no regulations on it, although many coats seem to have been double-breasted. The Army of Northern Virginia was a rather religious army, almost like Cromwell's New Model Army, and several waves of religious revivals, marked by baptisms of leading officers, swept it during the war.

G2 Hospital Steward, 1863

This steward is assigned to a regiment where his red badge on his hat marks him as being in the Infirmary Corps. He has acquired a green sash, mark of the Medical Corps in the U.S. Army, although it is not regulation. Many Confederate surgeons, too, wore green sashes.

G3 General Officer, 1864

The perfectly regulation uniform for generals and staff officers included a 'fore-and-aft' hat, rarely if ever seen. The regulation general, too, was to wear dark blue trousers with twin gold stripes and a buff sash. Lee wore such a sash when he surrendered at Appomattox.

H1 Private, 21st Mississippi Regiment, 1865

By 1865 the Confederate soldier was happy to get

A Baltimore, Maryland, engraver, Adalbert Johann Volck, produced this romantic impression of Stonewall Jackson leading his men at prayer during the war

any sort of clothing he could. Often they threw away their accoutrements, carrying only their blanket roll, haversack and canteen, often, as this one, captured from the enemy. Ammunition and caps were carried in trouser pockets.

H2 Major, 1st Regiment of C.S. Engineers, 1865

Officers in the Corps of Engineers were to wear 'fore-and-aft' hats like generals and staff officers. Their trousers were to be blue, but gray was more common. Facings in the engineers were white.

H3 First Lieutenant, C.S. Marines, 1865

Marines stationed round Richmond were part of the Army of Northern Virginia during the Appomattox campaign. They mostly wore blue *képis*, although a Marine Corps lieutenant wrote in 1863 from Richmond: 'Common gray caps are worth 12 to 14 dollars here. I got one this morning, a simple glazed cap, worth 30 cents, and paid $2.50 for it.' An original Marine Corps lieutenant's coat has army rank insignia on it and plain black trim. The gold 'Russian shoulder-knots' on each shoulder were not regulation Confederate, but used in the U.S. Marine Corps, and therefore used by C.S. Marine Corps officers much as they used U.S.M.C. buttons. The men wore accoutrements sent from England, '. . . such as used in the British service', while much of their clothing seems to have been supplied by army departments and consists of gray jackets and gray and white trousers.